This Journal

Belongs To:

_____

inspire

She
believed
SHE COULD
so she
did

Notes

_____

_____

_____

_____

_____

_____

_____

_____

_____

_____

Notes	*Notes*

Notes

Live
FOR
yourself

Notes

_____

_____

_____

_____

_____

_____

_____

_____

_____

_____

Notes	*Notes*

live
MORE
worry
LeSS

Notes

_____

_____

_____

_____

_____

_____

_____

_____

_____

_____

_____

_____

_____

_____

_____

_____

_____

_____

_____

_____

Notes

It's just a bad day, Not a bad life

Good
things
take
time

Notes

| Notes | Notes |

Notes

Live WHAT YOU Love

Notes

Passion
Over
Perfection

Notes

the best is yet to come

Notes

_____

_____

_____

_____

_____

_____

_____

_____

_____

_____

Notes	*Notes*

Notes

shine
bright

_____

_____

_____

_____

_____

_____

_____

_____

_____

_____

_____

_____

Notes	*Notes*

the universe is immaterial

Notes

_____

_____

_____

_____

_____

_____

_____

_____

_____

_____

_____

_____

_____

_____

_____

_____

_____

_____

Notes

Notes

Good things take time

Notes

Do what
makes
you
Happy

Notes

You become what you believe

Notes

Notes

Each failure
brings you
one step
closer to
success

Notes

IT ALWAYS SEEMS Impossible UNTIL IT'S DONE

_____

_____

_____

_____

_____

_____

_____

_____

_____

_____

_____

_____

_____

Notes	*Notes*

Notes

Notes

Live FOR yourself

Notes

_____

_____

_____

_____

_____

_____

_____

_____

_____

_____

_____

_____

Notes	*Notes*

live
MORE
worry
LeSS

Notes

every moment matters

Notes

It's just a bad day, Not a bad life

Good things take time

Notes

_____

_____

_____

_____

_____

_____

_____

_____

_____

_____

_____

Notes	*Notes*

Live
WHAT YOU
Love

Notes

Live
WHAT YOU
Love

Notes

Passion
Over
Perfection

Notes

Made in United States
Orlando, FL
03 March 2022

15353410R00057